Intimate Presence

Divinely Inspired Poetry
Inspired by Yeh-low

David Joseph Staab

First Printing: [2025]

ISBN: 979-8-9994390-2-4

Written by: David Joseph Staab
Published:
Vibe the Waves Publishing House LLC
www.VibetheWavesPublishing.com

Cover Design: Alannah Serbeck

Illustration Design: Michaela Shurts

Edited by: Rae Serbeck

Printed in the United States of America
Vibe the Waves Publishing House is a registered trademark of Vibe the Waves Publishing LLC

Contents

Intimate Presence

Divinely Inspired Poetry Inspired by Yeh-low

David Joseph Staab

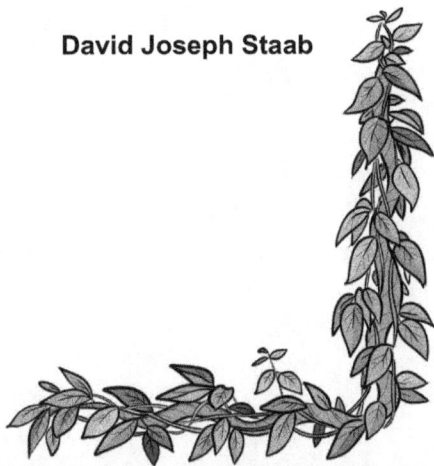

Preface

This is a collection of poems that came through me during the most transformative time in my life.

After leaving a heavily narcissistic marriage, God guided me through wild layers of healing. With each poem, I found myself at the depths of my unconscious mind, working through a lesson I needed to integrate in order to heal from my past.

This poetry book is also an unexpected journey. If you read closely, you'll notice the flow and shifts happening within me as the collection unfolds.

It begins with me diving deep into my own shadows—facing the things I allowed and enabled from a lack of self-love. Then it moves into my path of rediscovering that love for myself. And finally, it reaches a space I never expected: attracting the most beautiful, conscious, and healthy relationship I've ever experienced. Through this, I've come to truly understand what love is—after deeply discovering what it is not.

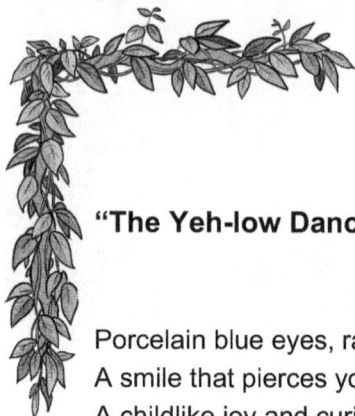

"The Yeh-low Dance"

Porcelain blue eyes, radiant red lashes,
A smile that pierces your heart in the softest ways.
A childlike joy and curiosity, observing the world around.
Emanating intimate presence,
When she feels the depth of her safety.

Dancing in Her Liberation.
For only God and Herself,
The most Divine Flow.
If you have the Eyes to See.

No external sign of the Wars won,
Within and Without,
That she bares in her Soul.
Only she Knows.

Your faults, stumbles, imperfections, shadows,
Observing without Judgment or Contempt.
Not to Enable,
But because of Her Faith
in your ability to Learn and Grow.

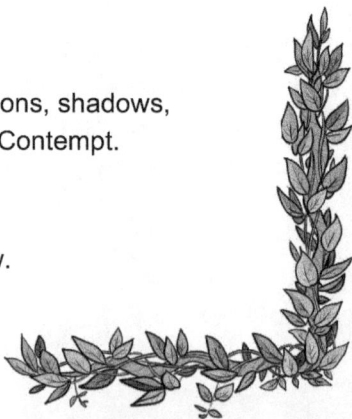

Giving the most gentle, pure love,
Willingly and openly.
As it's a reflection of the purity of her heart,
Rare beyond measure.

How God Expresses Himself through her,
Is my Favorite way.

Her divine team, watching and dancing with her always,
Angels on her left and right, above and below.
They came to me during Ayahuasca once,
I thanked them with my heart,
They smiled and knew this was Right.

What an honor it is.
To be the One she chooses,
To Give all the Love she's given,
To the world and those unworthy.
Right back to her mind, body, and Soul.

For her to be cherished, Seen, Heard, Touched,
In the most divine of ways.
As God knows the Love she's worthy of,
As does she, finally.

I pray God allows this dance to continue
throughout this lifetime.
Always surrendering to His plan, regardless
Only He knows and is the Arbiter of Truth and Love
So I will make the most of every moment spent
With this Sacred Yeh-low soul of Love, Joy,
Play, and Radiance

Thank you my Yeh-low.
For the divine showing,
Of what Love is, and Can Be.

I choose you, with All of Me.
I will always do my best,
To return it to you, in my most special ways.

"Pause"

Watch the mind and all the stories it creates,
What's real, what's not.
Does it even matter? You can't miss what's meant for you.

What's here and Now?
What feelings are arising in this moment?
If you can Pause long enough, more feelings will arise.
Those are the most real.

The ones we may not want to look at,
with a world of distractions,
They are so easy to bury.

Self love is the key they say, but in this world of duality,
How nice and rare it is to be gently loved by another,
With no motive
other than to experience gentle love itself.

How nice even, to be able to receive it Pause, and find your real. It's in there, waiting and guiding you to Love. The external will follow shortly thereafter.

Today, I hope you Pause.

And I hope I do too.

"Feel your Pain"

Feel to Heal,
Emotions suppressed from dark days.

Feel your disappointment,
From those you trusted taking advantage of you,
With no regard to your wellbeing.

Feel your Anger.
Anger is a mask for Sadness,
from being hurt by those you chose to love.

Feel your Resentment,
Towards those that wronged you.
Knowing in your heart,
they were deeply hurt by others.
But are choosing not to heal,
instead projecting their pain onto you.

Feel your pain, Feel it all, To let it all go, let
Them all go. Allowing new space for light
and peace, And new beings with a True
heart to enter.

You are Worthy of the Purest Love.

"The Dark Teacher"

Emasculating criticism.
Covertly Guiding you to your Worthiness,
UnGodly turmoil, emotional mental Spiritual Chaos,
Forcing the depth of your Strength within to Rise.

Daily, for Years,
Chiseling, sharpening you into the Being you Must become.
Every external emotional comfort ripped away, Nonexistent,
Leading you to the Deep Awareness of God Within.

Falling, again and again,
The Dark showing you all the ways you're not Enough.
Years of Tears only You will ever know,
Through the Darkness,
overcoming Demon after Demon,
Slowly, you Grow, then All At Once.

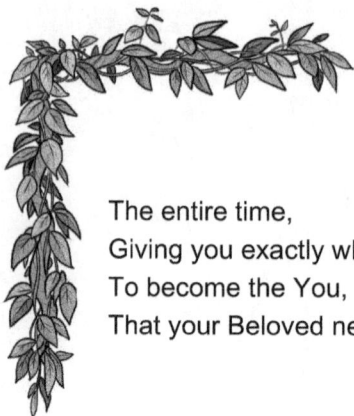

The entire time,
Giving you exactly what you asked for,
To become the You, that the World needs,
That your Beloved needs.

To become the You, that You need.

"The Beauty of Neglect"

Only experienced far after the dust settles,
The Darkest night
can only precede the sun's brightest Light.

A heart pure, desiring only Love.
Used for service to self, of those most trusted,
Covertly becoming the Source,
Of nothing the Pure Heart intended.
Conditioning, programming you to go without,
the Illusion of being OK.

Recklessly loving without Discernment,
Manifests the most painful,
yet essential Lessons Sacred to Life.

The Desire to Receive is ever prominent.
Yet Loving those who do not Cherish your Heart.
Along with your Allowing,
Enablement, lack of Self Worth,
Lethal combination of Love's Greatest Lessons.

Love is ever present internally, within.
In a world of Duality,
to go without the external weighs on your soul.
Stripped of all sensation of Touch, Comfort, Intimacy,
Becoming your greatest Enigma.

This passes, you then find those that truly See you,
As you can now See Yourself.
A chapter necessary for divine appreciation,
To be Cherished and loved in the
Deserving way you now Know.

When the Dark Night passes,
There is no Brighter Light than the Sun's Yeh-low Rays.

"Of Service or A Servant"

Are you of Service to someone, or are you A Servant?
Narcissism rampant in the world,
covertly seeking to Control,
Lack of appreciation the foundational sign of Servanthood,
Only you know, within You.

Meticulous methods conditioning You to be controlled.
Small, subtle, hyper effective,
Until automation sets in, Draining you Daily,
Outside of Breadcrumbs to keep Hope Alive.

It only Ends when you End it, fully.
Chaos ensuing even then,
When they can no longer control you,
They move to controlling what others think of You.

All in Divine orchestration.
To teach you the depths of what Love is not,
To teach you to Honor your heart,
To teach you the depths of appreciation,
When true Love does Come.

In Stillness of the mind, ask yourself,
Am I in Service Or am I a Servant?

"Pain"

What a wonderful teacher to inevitably experience.

Those that seem the most centered and loving,
have had to experience the depths of the opposite.

To experience the depths of the pain of loneliness,
Is to come to the Truth of the Living Divine within you,
Now and Forever.

To experience the pain
of how you don't deserve to be Loved,
Is to find your knowing
of the only Love you will accept.

To experience the pain of not being good enough,
Is to come to the truth
that you always were and will be.

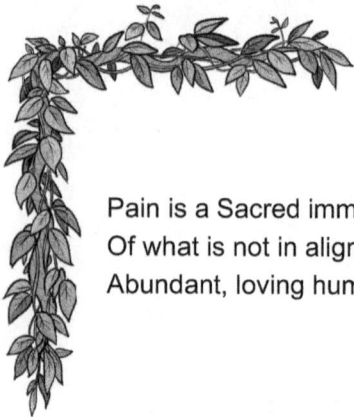

Pain is a Sacred immediate call to your awareness,
Of what is not in alignment for your most expansive,
Abundant, loving human experience.

To live a life avoiding pain, is to live a life of Suffering.

Welcome Pain, embrace its teachings with Full Surrender,
and continue to Expand,
More than you ever thought possible.

"Into Your Shadow"

You Go.

If it's Harmony and Inner Peace you truly Desire,
Within your Shadows, lies the path to your liberation.

What is the root of your insecurity?
What are the roots of your Attachments?

You are Whole and Complete, within each moment.

The Sacred Pause will allow,
The Arising Feelings to Guide your Way.
Lengthen the Sacred Pause, through the Discomfort,
To the Peaceful message of the Divine within.

Your Shadow is waiting, not to be discarded or shamed,
But to be Loved and Integrated.
Pause until the Shadow surfaces,
To show you where the Love within you is needed most.

The Love that is always there from God ,
And yearns to be Given.

By You.

"Shadows Lead the Way"

Shadows, Existing within us all,
Heavily judged, while being the Path to your Liberation.
Childhood wounds developed into core beliefs,
Creating disharmony in intimacy, connection, flow.

The sacred key is not to cast them away,
Separate mind from emotion, with gentle curiosity.
Remove projection upon the catalyst,
Most rooted in Not Being Enough.

Surfacing through our most intimate relationships,
Those not meant for us, will not hold the space.
Those meant for us, will do so with grace, Always
for you to discern within yourself.

Integration of the Shadows.
The Path to your most intimate
connected human experience,
Found only within the conscious Choice of your mind.
Only you know the conversations with You.

Befriend the discomfort of your deepest shadows.
Surrendering to the divine expansion that will follow.

"Concern has a Price"

Dancing with Ayahuasca in the Depths of her Wisdom.
She whispers to me "Concern has a Price",
Then leaves Leaving me to decode yet another,
One of her Sacred Teachings.

Concern.
One of the most beautiful,
yet overlooked examples of Prayer,
Yet every experience has a Shadow.

To Desire Concern of others,
Is to Desire others being a state of fear,
Not to shame the Desire,
But to look upon the root with curiosity
To choose not to,
Will continue Karmic cycles of suffering for Both.

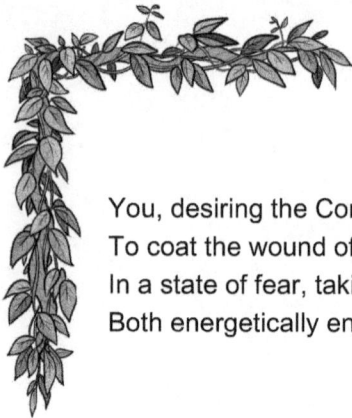

You, desiring the Concern of others,
To coat the wound of lack of self love Others.
In a state of fear, taking them out of their alignment of Faith,
Both energetically entangled in this Messy Dance.

The greatest insult to a Soul is to feel sorry for them.
The root message being "You can't handle this", Oh
but they can, and they will, if they Choose to.

Allow Concern to arise Authentically, Allow
it to be a beacon of light, In your journey
back to Unwavering Faith.

"Be With It"

Be with the Good feelings,
They will pass.
Be with the Bad feelings,
They will pass too.

Ride the waves of the ocean of life.
Detaching more and more,
From the belief that any wave is anchored to the sea floor,
For they are never ending,
connected to the Eternal Ocean.

Intentionally finding quiet peace in the in between,
Stilling the mind, slowing the breath.
Coming into your heart space,
This is your Sanctuary,
available to you in any moment.

Enjoy the ride, you're only here but a moment in time,
Everything you experience will pass one day.
If you can't enjoy it,
At least choose to Be With It.

"Choosing You"

The Desires of your Heart,
Align seamlessly,
When You finally choose You.

When You choose You,
Your most efficient Service follows,
As your Cup now overflows,
Rather than Serving on Empty.

The Spiritual Facade
Of self sacrifice
Masking Lack of Self Love
Glorifying suffering, unnecessary

Sacrifice is a necessary part of divine service,
But never intended to sacrifice,
To the depths of hindering the Self.

Patient gentle love is There,
Waiting for You to choose You,
A calm peaceful aligned life is There,
Waiting for You to choose you.

Your hearts deepest desires are There,
Waiting for You to choose You.

"Changing Seasons"

Everything's changing,
A little for so long, then everything all at once.
Everything you ever asked for, On The Way,
Hidden by uncomfortable unknowns and worldly shifts.

Tests of the depths of your Trust in God constantly present,
Coming back to your Knowing time and time again.
All is well, everything working out for you,
Now fast tracked, the gift of years of deep work.

The in between time of what was and what will be,
A necessary uncomfortable divine ride, unavoidable.
Putting all your tools to the test,
At the same time,
As simple as finding your breath and Heart Center.

When the shift is complete,
Everything you've ever dreamed of at hand,
Never as you expected, nor the way you expected it,
Yet perfect in every way.

"Looking for Problems?"

The mind, conditioned to navigate Chaos for years,
Takes time to settle into Peace.
Deepening your awareness,
especially when discomfort arises.
Is it Real?
Or are you searching,
operating on old programs of survival?

What you search for you will find,
The mind is great at making illusions real.
Just because it's real in your mind, Doesn't
mean it's rooted in the Highest Truth.

The more you let go of the fragile reality you once lived in,
The more the Highest Truth of your solid ground,
comes to your Knowing It will happen.
No matter what,
as it's now your Truth
It will happen more Harmoniously,
based upon the choices of your mind.

Daily rituals necessary during any major transition,
Still the mind or it will keep you racing,
Connect to nature, breath, walk slowly,
Smile, connect, and most of all, Play.

You are Worthy of all that is Here and Coming,
And you've never known this more,
So now it's here to Stay.

"You Were Enough"

All along.

The entire time. More than enough, actually.

The child within will tell you otherwise.
The innocence of your heart will take it on, willingly.
The mind ever determined to become "better"
will give you your answer to improve.

Missing the Sacred Truth all along.

You are More than enough, and always have been.
The creation of You
was molded in unique perfection.

The right person will reflect
this back to you effortlessly.

The right people will honor this in you,
gently reflecting back,
blind spots of innocent intention.

You were, and will always be, Enough.

"Purity of Love"

To truly know what Love is,
One must first know what Love is Not.
Uncomfortable necessity of Karmic Relationships,
To lead you to the Knowing of what you are Worthy of

Love is Not Angry, nor Harsh.
Love does not Blame, nor accuse.
Love is Gentle, even when direct.
Love seeks to understand, without needing to be Right.

Love is not intentionally harmful, nor aggressive.
Love does not seek to control, nor possess.
Love is Kind,
even when speaking an uncomfortable Truth.
Love accepts you as you are,
honoring your sovereignty.

Love accepts your shame, guilt, doubts and fears.
Love sees the Truth in them;
the scared child desiring love and safety.
Love honors its boundaries, ensuring.
Love is also treated with Love.
Love walks away, when Love realizes what Love is Not.

"Let it be Good"

You've mastered surviving in Chaos,
Can you now Master thriving in Peace?

The mind, always choosing a familiar hell,
Over an unfamiliar heaven.
Until the Spirit is truly ready to Receive Heaven,
Can you get comfortable in Peace?

Let the self sabotaging thoughts arise.
Giving them grace,
they kept you safe when it wasn't safe,
Letting them know they are no longer needed,
For now your Sanctuary is at hand.

You've come out of the battlefield,
war torn and scarred up,
Now your paradise awaits,
Here and Now,
If you can allow it.

"Profoundly Enough"

Diving Timing, Always Unexpected.

The Greatest Gift, to be Loved, simply for Being,
There is no Earning Love, when you're Profoundly Enough.

The sweetest Love unfolds,
Only in Deep Surrender of the Present Moment.

The connection deepens with every gentle word spoken,
Of past wounds still lingering.

Depth of Safety, immeasurable, Finally.

Pause.

Both with a knowing and readiness to receive
The Love Deserved.

To know what love is Not is one thing,
To know, Truly, what Love Is Divine,
Soft, Gentle, Conscious.

The Dance will continue,
Eternally in Moments.

As Two Choose, each day,
As God Allows.

Oh how I Pray,
The Yeh-low Dance continues On.

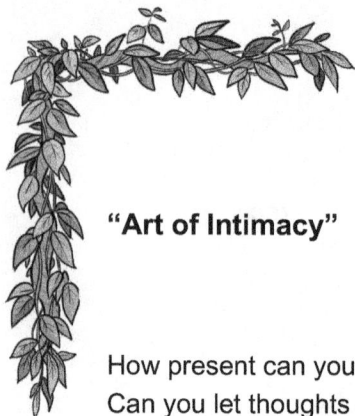

"Art of Intimacy"

How present can you be?
Can you let thoughts of What Comes Next,
go completely?

Fully immerse yourself in the moments sensation,
Allow unfolding naturally.
The thought of What Comes Next,
Creates the disconnect,
Taking back control from the divine surrender of perfect.

Can you sustain the Moment,
Keeping the mind at bay,
Releasing sensations of pressure or expectation?
It's ok if you don't, how else do we learn?

Foundations of Intimacy are Truth and Authenticity,
followed by Presence.
Disconnect also lies in deception and masks,
ill intentions.
All felt at an energetic level by the divine feminine.

Do you love yourself enough, to be Authentically you?
Start there.

"Be Too Much"

Because you're not.

Be the one that Loves too hard. That Dives too deep.

It's the only way to find the one that can and Will,
Match that Love.

Don't hold back.
Your Love is too unique, too special,
And Needed more than the world will ever let you know.

Put your heart out there, again and again.
Will pain come? Absolutely.
Pain will come to redirect you to a matched Love,
That yearns to openly Love,
Just as deep as you always have, and will.

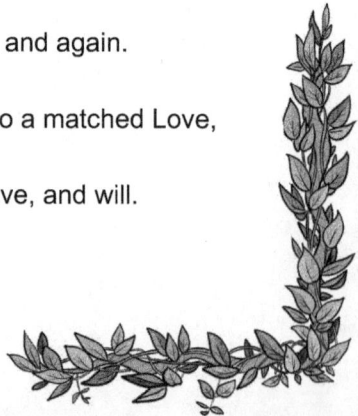

This life is but a Moment in time.
It will all pass.
It's passing even now as you read these words.

Be Too Much. Love too hard.

Because there is no such thing, To the
Heart that was Written for You.

"Strange Liberation"

Years of Unhealthy Dynamics,
Makes a Healthy Dynamic,
Initially strange.

What do you mean I'm enough just as I am?
Can't you see all the ways
my mind tells me I could be better?
You're not upset something didn't go as planned?
What is this sense of Flow & Acceptance,
Shouldn't something need to be fixed?

Just being here with Me is enough?
Shouldn't there be a need for More,
Greater Places and Shinier Things?
Do you Appreciate me? Openly and vocally?
I've only found appreciation within myself,
knowing I do what is Right.

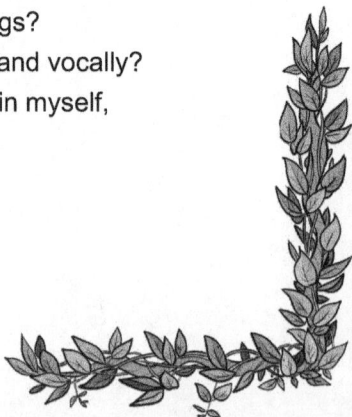

Strange Liberation,
Into the Love, Respect,
and Experience you have Deserved,
All along And now Love yourself enough,
To experience the Beauty
of it Symbiotically with Another,
On a strangely similar journey.

Now, Enjoy the Dance, Fully,
For the First Time.

"On The Other Side"

In The Beginning,
Wounds from your Mother and Father.

Reflected Divinely,
In your most challenging romantic endeavors.

The Monster you want to blame,
Is merely a reflection of the deepest work,
You must do within yourself.
To truly know your Worthiness of the Love you desire.

Not a Monster at all,
But a Sacred gift of the most uncomfortable kind.

Years of tears,
Pain, and abuse that only You will ever know.
Every second necessary for your souls request,
For the evolution at hand.

On the Other Side…

Oh how beautiful the world becomes.
How sacred each moment becomes.
How Intimate each touch becomes.

The Love you will Attract,
And be capable to Receive.

On The Other Side.

Is worth every second.

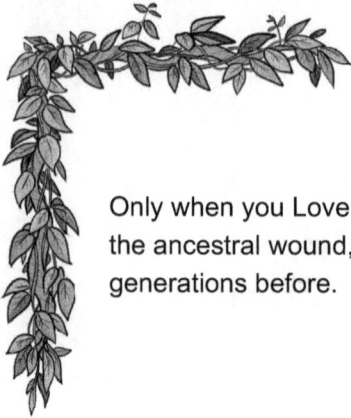

Only when you Love yourself enough, And heal the ancestral wound, That has plagued you and generations before.

Will you find yourself…..

On the Other side.

"Angels are with You"

When you stumble, when you fall.
When you Rise, and in the inbetween.

They cry with you, in those difficult moments,
Only You know about,
When you thought you were all Alone and Lost.
They laugh with you, when the Cosmic Giggle hits.

Observing, discreetly guiding your path.
Following their Divine Orders
to oversee your special mission.

Dropping little hints that can only be caught,
By present awareness.
Animals, feathers in a moments gaze, numbers,
So many other ways beyond our human knowledge.

The Love they have for You is immeasurable,
The gratitude they have for your decision to face the trials.
You are in this life for your Soul Growth,
And the Betterment of Humanity, even more so.

Angels are with you, even in this very Moment.

You are Never Alone.

"Freedom is the Path to Love"

Love is not Possessive
True Love is setting someone free
Self love is choosing the One
That chooses you with that Freedom

To truly experience the depths of love
You must set someone completely free
How else can they ever Truly choose you
By their own choice

To control or possess
Is to create energetic chains
Blocking the experience of their deepest Choice
As they are partially
choosing you from energetic obligation

To experience the fullness of Love
The choice must be made to fully choose each other
By each individual soul and mind
Which can only happen when two souls are Free

Set them free
And if it's meant to be, it Will Be

"Distrust to Disharmony"

Do you truly Trust those you Love?
Do those you Love,
Truly Trust you?
Distrust is the root of disharmony.

Distrust is the root of Controlling behavior
To attempt to control another
Is to disrespect the journey of their soul
And to show lack of Faith of God within them.

Trust even if they fail,
As the failures are some of Gods greatest blessings.
In the journey of the Soul Evolving,
Do you not wish them to learn and grow?

Does God wish his child to be forever dependent,
Upon Him?
Or to step into the sovereign nature,
That was seeded within at birth?

The more one Trusts, the relationship will flow
The more one distrusts, Disharmony ensues

Let It Be

"Freedom"

Divine Flow of Service,
Connection, Intimacy
Comes only through One Way
Being Authentically You.

Some will go their entire Human Experience
trying to fit into a Box
Of another's wounded expectation
Failing even at that.

Pressure, Judgements.
All subconscious , felt all the same
Creating constant distortions of your Authentic nature
Ironically blocking the deepest desires of your Heart

To force
is to create the illusion of scarcity of love
To allow
Is to surrender and know
A sacred key to recieving

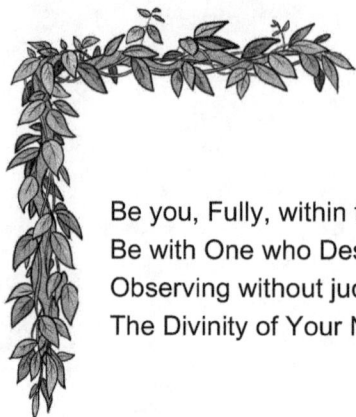

Be you, Fully, within first
Be with One who Desires only the Authentic You
Observing without judgement
The Divinity of Your Nature

Then, Enjoy the Dance

"Good Doesn't Always Feel Good"

Uncomfortable conversations with those you love.
Rooted in authenticity and truth.
Stilling the mind, daily,
When life's distractions are never ending.

Choosing vulnerability,
When the heart wants to close,
Taking the leap of your hearts desire,
While your mind
gives you every fear and potential failure.

Listening to your loved one
express their uncomfortable Truth.
Allowing the pain to rise, settling into it, being with it.
If you really love them, you'll want their
Truth over your Desire.
If they really love you, they will want the same.

Letting others hate and judge you,
projecting their internal world
Letting go of all attachment
that arises with the pain of being human
Falling into a deeper Knowing, that You know your Heart
As does God, that's all that really matters.

Good doesn't always feel Good.

"Intimate Presence"

Let it all go,
The doubts,
The fears,
The worries.

Let go.
Of any opinion or action.
Of anyone,
That doesn't see your value.

There's a difference between someone liking you,
and someone that sees your value.
Keep those that truly See you close,
Let Go of the rest.

Let go of the attachments
Of putting your happiness
in the hands or words of another.
Let it all go.
When you do this, you're back Home.

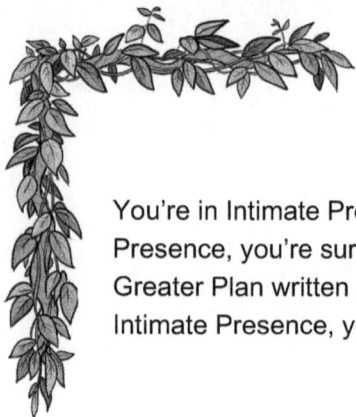

You're in Intimate Presence. In Intimate Presence, you're surrendered, To the Greater Plan written perfectly for you, In Intimate Presence, you're with God.

Let it all go, and it all will come.

"The Inbetween"

Everything's changing,
One chapter closes,
Another Opening

The perfect messiness of the Puzzle
Waiting to be put back together
Patience, Presence, Faith,
All so necessary

Letting the old programming burn away,
So the new can Flourish.
Allowing many souls to fade away,
those that cannot Discern,
Manipulation from Truth
No longer room for those that doubt Your Heart
Eyes open to what Love is not,
Revelations of the Beauty of what Love is

Tests, will you Pass?
It's ok if you don't
If you do, Profound Expansion awaits

Letting go of Force, Allow the Divine Unfolding
Hands off the wheel, finally, All in the hands of God

How beautiful will you Now Allow life to become?

"Sail Away"

To a Realm of Peace.
A Sanctuary of Kindness and the Sweetest Love,
Existing within the Eternal Moment, Now Full Surrender,
releasing the Mind Thoughts.

Sail Away

To a Realm of Divine Safety
Where suttle Vulnerabilities and Past Wounds gently arise,
To be Held then lovingly released.
Where Receiving is effortless, and Serving is pure Joy.
Never ending, within each Moment.

Sail Away

To a Realm of Passion,
Intimate Connection,
matched only by Intimate Presence.
Every Touch, Like it is the First and Last, All at once.

Sail Away with me

Again Soon

"Roots of Pressure"

The Kryptonite of Man.
Pressure, Covertly blocking
the Divine expression within.

Shadowy Roots,
Needing Control,
Inadequacy, doubting the Self,
Lack of Faith in God.

Coming upon Moments of perceived importance.
The Paradox exists,
Let go to Release the Pressure,
As it's Always in God's Perfect hands.

A necessary journey,
Leading you to Unwavering Faith in yourself.
In the Written Orchestration
of your Human Experience,
And the Divine expressing Himself, through you,
In each moment.

The Suffering of Pressure is self inflicted,
The Liberation of Pressure can also only come from the Self.

"God Knows Your Heart"

Care not of any other beings opinion.
God knows your heart,
If your Heart is True,
What else could matter?

People can only meet you
as deeply as they have met themselves,
Most lacking depth from traumas, distorted belief systems.
No fault of their own, No judgement against them.

To attach to criticism, Is to Deny the Only Truth that matters,
Only you know your path,
The Divine sees into the Truth of every being.

Humans do not Know Truth,
They Know their experience,
Which can never be your experience,
Your path is unique to You and God, alone.

In the end, all darkness comes to light.
The Truth and those that live Truly, Will
always Stand.

"Be to Attract"

Need for nothing, Gain Everything,
Reach in desperation, push it far away.

Be Still and Know, Everything Aligns Perfectly, Allow
distractions to control the mind, Chaos ensues.

Full presence in the sacred moment, Intimacy expands,
A thought of What Comes Next, disconnect follows.

Aligned action with Full Surrender,
Harmony experienced,
Forced action with necessity of control,
Disharmony develops.

How deeply can you Trust the divine
unfolding in each moment that is to come.
While being fully Present in the Sacred Gift of Now?

"Love is Not"

Harsh.

There is beauty in Harsh being masqueraded as Love.

It's found in the journey of the Soul,
Steadily recognizing what Love is Not.

The mind will justify it,
Grasping to the initial story that seeded,
The hooks of this false love.
But Truth always prevails, eventually, one way or another.

It could take days, years, a lifetime or a few. The
story will play out differently for each being.

But in any moment the veil can be lifted, to see,
The truth that cannot be unseen.

Love is Not Harsh.
Feeding into the illusion of necessity of Control is.

Rooted in fear, and imaginative scarcity of love.

To learn what Love is Not, is to learn what Love is.

"Follow the Fear"

Life's greatest expansions,
Found in the depths of suppressed fears within our mind.
Seeded, growing, creating anxiety and disconnection,
The more avoided, the more they gain power.

If avoided long enough, the fear may even come to life,
To show you a deeper lesson
of everything always working out.
Even if the fear is true,
It doesn't make it detrimental to life, as our mind will tell us.

Most often fear is an illusion,
Though feeling quite real within you.
There's only one way to expand beyond it and conquer it,
Bring it to surface,
Sit with it, be with it, stare it in the eyes directly.

If you're truly committed to expansion in your life,
Follow your Fear
Trusting in God's plan above all,
And watch it disappear before your very eyes.

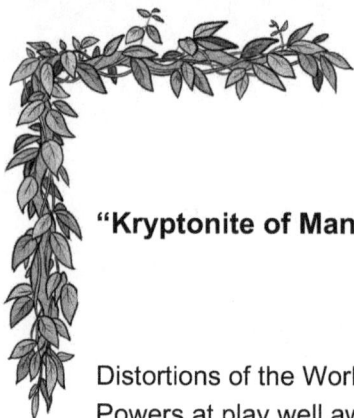

"Kryptonite of Man"

Distortions of the World, Heavily created by Downfall of Men.
Powers at play well aware,
Heavens Angels praying for change.

Men are intentionally controlled by one of two factors, or both.
Inability to control Sexual Energy, Inability to become Humble,
To Know they do Not Know.

Corruption of Sexual energy,
The quickest way of Man's Fall,
To energetically cast the Sacred as Not Sacred,
Felt at the deepest levels by the divine feminine,
The Great Destroyer of true Intimacy and connection.

Arrogance to think He Knows Best,
Unconsciously saying He Knows better than God.
The Inability to listen
to the Intuition of a Divine Feminine,
With a Pure Heart.
Laying the groundwork, brick by brick,
To his own human Demise.

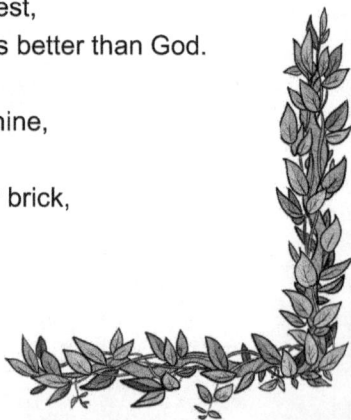

The only way back to the Light,
Love and grace for the Self,
A truly humble heart, quieting the Ego,
Listening to the Divine,
Extreme accountability and ownership,
with Inspired Action.

The Victim within must leave,
for the Victor within to Rise

"Rising Prayer"

God, continue to guide me as you always have,
Protect me as I continue the work I've been sent to do.

More importantly

Continue to help me get out of my own way,
And to better hear your messages, signs, and guidance

And to embody your love, Daily

"Who's Your Villain?"

Who comes to mind first?
How were you Wronged?

Evading a deeper question.

What Role have you played in Your Own Suffering?

Blame the Villain.

Evading the Sacred Truth.
The only Villain,
Is within,
Being projected upon another,
Parts of us we refuse to look at or
take accountability for.

There is no external Villain.

Acceptance of this, brings the opportunity for Harmony.

Play the game of blame,
Eternally suffer.

Feel the pain of self responsibility,
Welcome the Liberation, within and without.

You are Your Villain.

"Love, Expressed"

Your Love Expressed to another is capped
Or elevated based upon;

Your awareness and Depth of Presence,
In the Moments with them.

Your awareness of your own Shadows,
Amount of truth you're willing
to accept about your Shadows,
And ability to integrate them.

The compassion and Love of Self you have within.

Your communication and relationship with the Living
Divine.

The Safety you feel in your body from within yourself.

The Safety the Other being has created within themselves,
As you feel this unconsciously.

"Identity of Arrogance"

Spiritual superiority is delusion,
Pandemic within most communities,
To know you know, is to not know,
To know you don't know, is to know.

You cannot know anything outside of the self,
Even that is ever expanding and changing.
To judge another's situation,
Is only leading your spirit astray.

Many mistake belief for identity,
This is where the Fall begins.
If One is offended at conflicting information,
They have sold their soul to their identity.

Necessity of control and fear at the root,
Arrogance is where all Growth Ends.

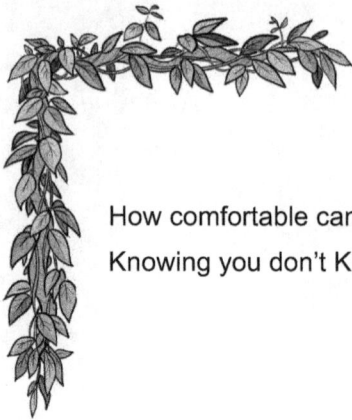

How comfortable can you become,
Knowing you don't Know?

"Paradox of Life"

Deeper into Pain, Deeper into Love.

Deeper into Solitude, Deeper into Authenticity.
The inverse is true too.

Reach, Chase, and it will Run.

Be, while in true Contentment of Self, Attract.

Accept the Pain, for the Pain to Release.

All in Divine Orchestration, All honoring your
Free Will.

Humble Love of Self, Attracts the True Love
of Another.

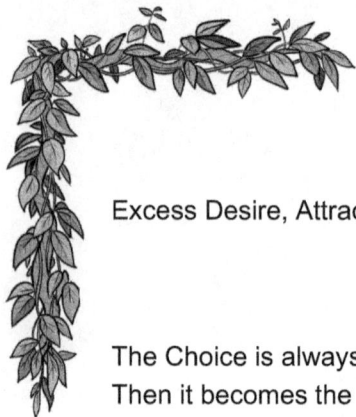

Excess Desire, Attracts Lessons rooted in Wounds.

The Choice is always yours, Until Divine Surrender.
Then it becomes the Best Choice.

"Shadows in a Healthy Mirror"

Shadows, ever prevalent in Mirrors
Unhealthy and Healthy,
Unhealthy Mirrors,
showing you where you're not Choosing You.
Healthy Mirrors,
giving the chance to deepen Love and Intimacy,
Healthy Mirrors come when Unhealthy Mirrors
Lessons Integrated.

Sit in the rising discomfort,
Without projecting upon the Love in front of you.
Bring it back to You,
Curiously observing the old story
being told within your mind.
Vulnerably communicate,
As that is where strength and transformation lies.
Fight the desire to self sabotage,
Ignoring the old story
telling you that is how you'll be safe.

Have your past wounds created Anxious
Or Avoidant attachment?
The Divine Experience,
Of Secure Attachment is Now Available,
If you can Allow it.

You are Whole and Complete.
You are Enough exactly as you are,
The right Love will see and reflect this,
As your knowing deepens within.

You are Whole and Complete,
You are Enough exactly as you are.

"Flow"

Breathe in, slow, feeling the air enter the nose,
Release, slowly, intentionally, feeling the air leave.

Flow- only found in Intimate Presence of This Moment,
Only continued by your Allowing.

Tension is the Antithesis of Flow,
Held in our shoulders,
Breathing in the Chest.

Automated distractions keeping Flow at bay,
Scrolling in comparison,
Worrying of a Future that's not real.
Fearing the patterns of old wounds being repeated.

Pause,
Breathe in, slow, feeling the air enter the nose,
Release, slowly, intentionally, feeling the air leave,
All is Perfect, in this Now Moment.

Here you are

"Love, Unconditional or Conditional"

I Love you If,
Or,
I Love you, Simply that.

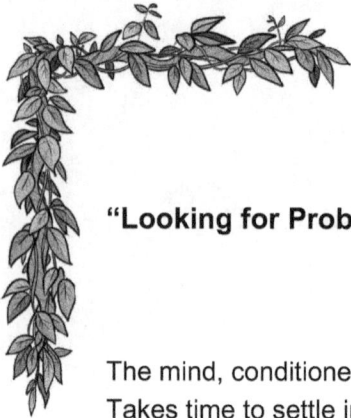

"Looking for Problems"

The mind, conditioned to navigate Chaos for years,
Takes time to settle into Peace.
Deepen your awareness,
especially when discomfort arises Is it Real?
Or are you searching,
Operating on old programs of survival?

What you search for, you will find.
The mind is great at making illusions real,
Just because it's real in your mind,
Doesn't mean it's rooted in the Highest Truth.

The more you let go of the fragile reality you once lived,
The more the Highest Truth,
Of your solid ground comes to your Knowing,
It will happen no matter what, as it's now your Truth.
It will happen more harmoniously,
based upon the choices of your mind.

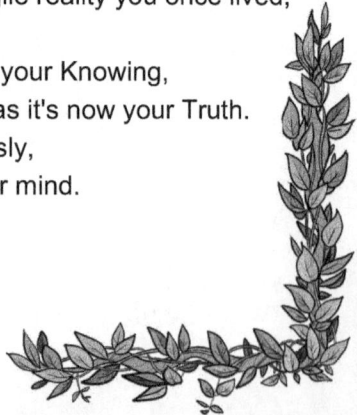

Daily rituals necessary during any major transition,
Still the mind or it will keep you racing.
Connect to nature, breath, walk slowly,
Smile, connect, and most of all, Play.

You are Worthy of all that is Here and Coming,
And you've never known this more,
So now it's here to Stay.

"Masculine Leadership"

The balance of embodying complete safety
And loving efficient direction
At its core,
This is what matters.

When men close their hearts,
Not allowing themselves to feel.
They see the feminine's emotions as wrong,
Something to be fixed Furthest from the Sacred Truth,
Creating disconnection and karmic lessons for both.

Truly strong men are Gentle men,
Taking aggressive action only when necessary.
To Protect, or do what is Right,
Without a need for validation,
But a Warrior within, available to do so at any moment.

Mastery of the Mind necessary,
Spiritual connection to a Higher Power necessary.
Mastery of Sexual energy is necessary,
it cannot control you. Mastery of Self Responsibility,
And vocal Personal Boundaries necessary.

Not an easy road for men in today's world,
Heavily disregarded, unappreciated by most,
Temptations and pitfalls at every corner.

But the Warriors will Rise, regardless.

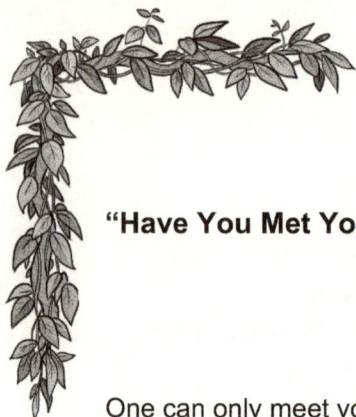

"Have You Met Yourself?"

One can only meet you,
At the depths at which they've met themselves.
One can only Love you,
At the depths at which they've learned
to Love themselves.

Manipulators, deceivers, those with Ill Intentions,
Can not believe your Authentic Loving heart exists.
Forever finding a way to paint
you as the darkness within them,
To bring them temporary false peace
in their world of Illusions.

Don't expect One to know,
The Lessons of facing your Shadows,
When they are not yet ready,
To peak into their own Eternal projections, Victimhood,
So much more appealing To those not ready to See,
Deeper Truths within themselves.

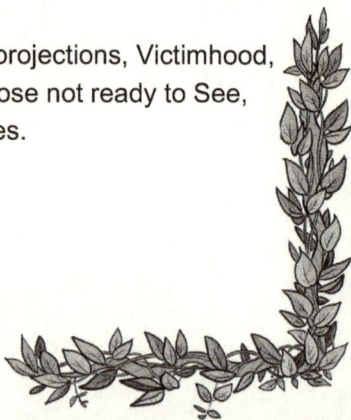

Your light, a constant reminder,
Of the Work they refuse to do.
Allow those who leave your experience to leave,
Making room for Divinely aligned souls.

How deeply have you met Yourself?

"Guerrero Espiritual"

The Spiritual Warrior,
Usually standing alone,
Or with few others,
Also daring to go to the depths of themselves.

How Humble can you become,
While standing morally & ethically firm?
Unwavering in your commitment to God, Service, & Love.

Overcoming the Maya's temptations for a Higher Calling.
Greed, Lust, Hate, Disdain for others, Pride,
Giving any power to opinions outside your own,
Gods, and your Beloveds.
Staying rooted in the Truth of your Soul & Heart.

How deeply do you consent,
To God's Sharpening of your Sword?
Do you Allow or Resist His fortifying of your Shield?
Necessary discomforts,
For a Harmonious Life of efficient Service Love,
At the core of every uncomfortable experience.

You are the One your ancestors Prayed for.

"Healing Journey"

The healing process
Messy as it can be
Essential, to sit in the ancestral burning
Of those that walked before you
That carried what you are choosing to Finally Release

Light casted upon every shadow
Insecurities brought to surface
Necessary discomfort to find your deepest
Truth Of the perfection of You

You can become a monk and sit on a mountain forever,
Isolated
The easy path to enlightenment
But to open your heart to another
To bare yourself, Naked in all ways
This Risk, this Daring act
The only way to unearth the deepest layers

Gods grandest creation
Your gentle loving heart
Awaits the life of harmony and flow
Only found
Through your deepest courage and action

Of your Healing Journey

"My Prayer"

Oh God, Creator of my Soul,
Continue to Protect and keep me Safe,
To Serve the purpose you have placed upon my Heart.

Continue to teach me the depths of Love,
To Love those that don't know how,
with boundaries necessary.
Bring me to Perfection,
In Love expressed to your Yeh-low Child.

Give me Strength,
To continue to fight the battles
You've sent me to fight,
In realms unseen by human eyes.

Be with me Always, To my Last breath,
As you've been with me since my first,
Until you call upon me Again,
To do your Beautiful Work.

Thank you Eternally,
For all you've done, and Will do,
In every way, I am Surrendered to your righteous Hand.

If these words touched your heart in any way, please share this book with at least one other soul in your life - someone also on their journey of discovering what Love truly is to them.

About the Author

David is a seasoned and gifted shaman with nearly a decade of profound experience working with Ayahuasca. Over the years, he has successfully guided thousands on his transformative healing journeys, leading life-changing Ayahuasca ceremonies that have touched lives and helped individuals heal on deep, multidimensional levels.

With a wealth of wisdom, David understands the intricate workings of the conscious, subconscious, and unconscious mind, as well as the interconnectedness of the physical, energetic, and spiritual bodies. His insight into the complexities of human healing goes far beyond surface knowledge, bringing clarity and empowerment to those they guide.

Having lived and trained in the heart of the Amazon jungle with revered elders on the Ayahuasca path, David has been deeply immersed in ancient healing practices and teachings. His work, grounded in both profound wisdom and personal experience, offers a unique and powerful perspective on personal growth and spiritual awakening. David continues to mentor and coach individuals on their journey to inner peace, alignment, and healing.

You can follow him and his journey on any of the following platforms;

Tiktok @shamanstaab
Instagram @shamanstaab

Thank You

www.ingramcontent.com/pod-product-compliance
Lightning Source LLC
Chambersburg PA
CBHW021201020426
42331CB00003B/154